J. R Eastwood

Poems for Little People

J. R Eastwood

Poems for Little People

ISBN/EAN: 9783744712873

Printed in Europe, USA, Canada, Australia, Japan

Cover: Foto ©Thomas Meinert / pixelio.de

More available books at **www.hansebooks.com**

Poems for Little People.

BY

J. R. EASTWOOD.

" . . . . To mould and fashion
Life's plastic newness into grace :
To make the boyish heart heroic,
And light with thought the maiden's face."
WHITTIER.

LONDON:
SIMPKIN, MARSHALL, HAMILTON, KENT & CO.

1891.

Second Edition.

*Printed at the "Pioneer Press"
By John Robb & Co., Liverpool.*

TO

RICHARD THOMAS HOLLAND

THESE VERSES

ARE GRATEFULLY INSCRIBED.

PREFACE.

The Poems and Songs contained in this volume have been, for the most part, already submitted to the judgement of the Public through the world-wide medium of "Cassell's Magazine," "The Quiver," "Little Folks," and "Cassell's Saturday Journal," and the author is indebted to the courtesy of Messrs. Cassell & Co., Limited, the Proprietors of these periodicals, for the privilege of presenting them in a collected form.

He also has pleasure in thanking the publishers of "Temple Bar," "London Society," "The Girl's own Paper," and "St. Nicholas" (Century Co., New York), for kind permission to reprint verses which he has contributed to these magazines.

Many of the Poems have been illustrated and set to music by eminent artists and composers. Among the former may be mentioned, F. Dicksee, A.R.A., M. E. Edwards, R. Barnes, Alice Havers, Percy Tarrant, Towneley Green, and W. Small; and among the latter, J. W. Elliot, J. W. Hinton, M.A., Mus. D., Frederick G. Cole, L. Mus., J. F. Bridge, Mus. D., Humphrey J. Stark, Mus. D., Hamilton Clarke, Mus. B., J. Gordon Saunders, and E. H. Turpin.

CONTENTS.

	PAGE
The Children	1
"Love me, Jessie!"	2
The Babes in the Boat	4
The New Baby	6
A Lullaby	8
Shortening the Baby	10
The March of the Geese	12
Jessie's Trouble	14
What the Birds are Singing	16
Dorothy	17
Father's Story	18
What the Birds teach us	20
In the Village Street	21
Jessie	22
Tired of Play	25
Ruth and Her Flowers	27
A Christmas Carol	29
Waiting for Father	30
The Children's Christmas	32
Bertie	34
Violets	35

CONTENTS.

	PAGE
Baby Collins	36
Baby	37
Their Little Queen	38
A King Deposed	40
The Child and the Mouse	42
Playmates	44
Harvest	46
The Old Mill	48
A Portrait	49
The Village Wedding	51
The Shoeing Forge	53
An English Girl	55
The Village May-day	57
Walter	59
An Unbidden Guest	61
The Singer	62
Thanksgiving	64
A Girl's Story	66
Constance	68
In the Cathedral	69
Muffled Music	73
Beyond Recall	74
"When I was a Boy!"	76
Vain Regrets	77
The Robin	79
Song	81
In Days to Come	82
The Golden Wedding	84
Far Apart	86
Desolate	88

CONTENTS.

	PAGE
Rondel	90
The Days Gone By	91
Faith and Work	93
Conscience	94
Let us be True	95
"The Evil Days"	96
"Dieu et mon droit"	98
Mariana	100
The Heart's Winter	102
Minor Chords	103
Confession	105
Grey and Blue	106
First Love	110
Twilight	111
The Rose	112
The Trysting Place	114
My Love and I	115
Sunset	117
Evening	118
The Bird's Message	119
Treasures	120
Betrothal	121
The Glade	122
Waiting	123
Hope Deferred	124
A Withered Rose	125
Starlight	127
Recompense	129
Consummation	130
Final Faith	132

CONTENTS.

	PAGE
Parting	133
Firelight	134
Rondel	135
Song	136
Lux in Tenebris	137
"No Cross, no Crown"	139
The City's Litany	141
Jubilee National Anthem	143
A Requiem	145
Emblems	148
"Vive l'Empereur!"	151
The Cross of the Legion of Honour	153
The Old Guard at Waterloo	156
Marshal Ney	159
Plevna, 1877	162
The King's Messenger	163

SACRED POEMS:

"For so He giveth His beloved sleep"	166
"Thou knowest not now!"	168
"Seek ye My Face!"	169
"For me to live is Christ, to die is gain"	170
"I stand at the door, and knock!"	172
"Our Father"	174
"Give Me thine heart!"	175
"Lovest thou Me?"	176
In Simon's House	178
Our Home Above	179
Forgiveness	180
The New Excelsior	181

THE CHILDREN.

IN breezy meadows where the sun
   Is seen without a cloud,
The happy, happy children run,
   And play, and sing aloud.

And I, who love all sights on earth,
   All sounds, revealing joy,
Would crown a thousand days with mirth
   For every girl and boy.

For soon, too soon, the days depart,
   And soon the golden hair
Is touched with snow, and mind and heart
   Too soon are filled with care.

So let the little children run,
   And play, and sing aloud,
In smiling meadows where the sun
   Is seen without a cloud.

"LOVE ME, JESSIE!"

"LOVE me, Jessie!" I heard one day,
    Watching the children at their play:
She was a baby girl, and he
A rosy, blue-eyed boy of three.

And some small grief had made her cry;
And Bertie pushed his playthings by,
In deep concern—but sure of this,
That all she wanted was a kiss.

And Jessie turned her tear-stained face,
And smiled to meet the boy's embrace;
And soon the childish tears were dried:
The little heart was satisfied.

"Love me, Jessie!" I heard him say;
And I should like to find a way
To make the sweet words live in rhyme
For children in the future time.

"LOVE ME, JESSIE!"

That every boy may kinder grow
In word and deed: for this I know,
That Kindness since the world began
For more than strength has made the man.

That little girls, however small,
May copy Jessie one and all;
And they will find, through all the years,
That love, sweet love, will dry their tears.

THE BABES IN THE BOAT.

WILLIE was two years old,
   And bright-eyed Minnie three,
And five and six, and good as gold,
   Were Tom and Margery.

These small folk loved to roam
   The shore, and dig the sand,
And Kate, our eldest girl at home,
   Was always close at hand.

Now once—this tale is true—
   They nearly got afloat,
Minnie, and baby Willie too,
   And in a fishing boat!

These trots had climbed, you see,
   Into this boat before
The tide came creeping quietly
   And rippling up the shore.

"Oh, let us pull the rope!"
  Cried Tom—"Pull, Peggy, pull!"
And with distress, and fear, and hope
  Their little hearts were full.

Kate heard the sudden cry,
  And in an instant came,
And brought the trots out, safe and dry,
  And no one got the blame!

THE NEW BABY.

OUR baby has the sweetest name:
We call him Noël, for he came
When snows were deep, and hearts were gay,
And joys were planned for Christmas Day.

His little face is like the moon:
He coos the same sweet wordless tune
Whose charm has touched our hearts before:
And every day we love him more!

He holds a Court of Love, and he
Controls and rules the nursery:
And now the days are never dull,
Because he makes them beautiful.

And all unquestioned, and untried,
This monarch small is satisfied
That all the love he gets is true,
And takes the homage as his due.

THE NEW BABY.

"I want to kiss him!" every day
We hear his little sisters say;
And baby stares with solemn eyes
While safe on mother's knee he lies.

And this is our new baby, he
Who sweetly rules the nursery:
Our Noël, born when hearts were gay,
And fields were white for Christmas Day.

A LULLABY.

THE waxen doll that shuts her eyes
  Is in her cot, and quiet lies;
And baby, flushed like any rose,
On mother's knee more wakeful grows:
She will not sleep, although I try
To soothe her with sweet lullaby—
      Sweet lullaby!

The battered horse, the broken dray,
The coral bells, are put away;
And baby, in her clean white gown,
On mother's breast may nestle down:
O hush, my darling, while I try
To sing to you sweet lullaby—
      Sweet lullaby!

Good night, to dear Red Riding Hood,
The pretty Children in the Wood:
And baby, free from all alarms,

Is rocked to sleep in mother's arms,
And will not waken, while I try
To bring sweet dreams with lullaby—
    Sweet lullaby!

SHORTENING THE BABY.

OUR baby now is four months old,
   A bonnie boy with hair like gold;
And his long clothes are put away,
For mother shortened him to-day.

He has the loveliest of frocks,
All trimmed with lace, and two pink socks
That father bought, the best by far
And prettiest in the whole bazaar.

And now the rogue can kick about:
His little feet go in and out
As though they could not rest, and he
Is just as happy as can be.

Besides, he feels quite proud to-day,
With all his long clothes put away,
And dressed so fine, and then, you know,
We praise the boy, and love him so!

His grandmamma must see him soon:
We all will go this afternoon,
And take the pet, and stay for tea;
And what a riot there will be!

At first, perhaps, she may not know
The baby, he is altered so:
But let her guess, and do not say
That mother shortened him to-day!

THE MARCH OF THE GEESE.

THE geese go marching through
   The farm-yard every day,
And down the meadows, two and two,
   They wander far away.

With all they chance to meet,
   A cackling noise is heard,
And waddling on with clumsy feet,
   They really look absurd!

And yet their foolish noise
   Brings back a tale to me,
That all should read, both girls and boys,
   Who study history.

The geese of ancient Rome
   Once cackled with affright,
When spoilers of the hearth and home
   Crept up the steep at night.

With clamour loud and shrill,
  From those high walls, they made
The waking hero's heart to thrill,
  While foes shrank back afraid!

I think that every one,
  Who reads this tale, will say
That even foolish geese have done
  Good service in their day.

JESSIE'S TROUBLE.

AROUND the doorway, fresh and green,
  The thick, bright ivy-leaves were seen;
And little Jessie, tired with play,
Sat on the step to rest one day.

A rosy maid of three or four,
She used to play about the door,
And go on journeys down the lane,
With Pussy, and come home again.

With curls unbonnetted, she sat
And nursed the little lazy cat;
And Pussy purred quite loud, for she
Felt warm and snug on Jessie's knee.

And now in Jessie's big brown eyes
A troubled look began to rise;
When she went out she had it on:
Oh, dear! where had her bonnet gone!

JESSIE'S TROUBLE.

And mother told her to be good,
And she, poor child, had said she would,
And kept herself so clean all day;
And now—oh! what will mother say?

But cheer up, Jessie! never mind!
When mother looks she soon will find
The bonnet lying in the lane,
And bring back all your smiles again!

WHAT THE BIRDS ARE SINGING.

THE music wanting words
   Is everywhere about
Where tender-throated Birds
   Fly softly in and out
Among the fir-trees high,
   With branches sere and brown,
That veil the autumn sky,
   And drop their needles down.

The faint and curious smell
   Of fir-cones on the ground
(Who does not know it well?)
   Is fragrant all around;
And everywhere the Birds,
   From branch and bough above,
In strains like sweetest words,
   Are singing, "God is love!"

DOROTHY.

A LITTLE rogue, and mother's pet,
   She cannot say her letters yet,
And, full of fun, she seldom tries,
With mischief dancing in her eyes.

But still our darling can behave
As good as gold, and look as grave
As if the business and the care
Of all the State were laid on her.

And she believes her friends are true
And good, and she will love them too;
And may she wear these graces long,
The faith and love that think no wrong!

Oh, happy child, what books can teach,
Or lips of wisdom strive to preach,
That we may learn, from hearts like thine,
To make these graces burn and shine!

FATHER'S STORY.

NOW, listen while I tell to you
   A story that is really true;
It is about a box, when we
Were children in the nursery.

High on the garden bank it stood,
An old square box of painted wood;
And there, in summer, we could play
At "Coach and Horses" every day.

Now this was years and years ago,
When father was a boy, you know;
And Auntie Florence was so small
I had to mind she did not fall.

Most children have to sit inside,
But on the box seat we could ride,
And hold the whip and reins, and see
The big horse trotting steadily.

We had no real horse, you know,
Though we, of course, pretended so,
Like other folk, with better sense,
And quite grown up, who make pretence.

And often, too, these folk could tell
They do not manage things so well,
Nor feel so happy every day
As little children in their play.

WHAT THE BIRDS TEACH US.

NOVEMBER now is here,
   With skies of leaden hue,
And gloomy days and drear,
   And winds that pierce us through.

And on the hedge the rose,
   With leaves of tender green,
No more in beauty grows,
   And frost and snow are seen.

But still the Birds contrive,
   By hardship unsubdued,
To keep themselves alive,
   And keenly seek their food.

And thus they teach us still,
   However dark the day,
"That where there is a Will
   There always is a Way."

IN THE VILLAGE STREET.

I MEET her in the village street:
   A pretty little maiden sweet,
With shy blue eyes, and forehead fair
And bright with blown and golden hair.

And since I only live to love
While earth beneath and skies above
Are bright by day and dark by night,
I meet and greet her with delight.

And sweet she is as sweet can be;
And till the heart that throbs in me
Is cold to beauty and to grace,
I shall rejoice to see her face.

For years of grief have rolled away
Since life grew dark one smiling day—
When Jessie died—but still I meet,
And clasp and kiss her in the street!

JESSIE.

I.

To me all beauty of the race
  Was in the beauty of her face;
And brightest gold would ill compare
With brightness of her golden hair!

Sweet as the blue of summer skies,
The rare blue of her roguish eyes;
Sweet as a rosebud from the south,
The marvel of her perfect mouth!

And words of wonderment were weak,
Of all her winning ways to speak,
Whose graciousness had fairer grace
Than all the fairness of her face!

Alas! that I shall hear no more
Her footsteps light upon the floor,
And that my lips must sadly miss
The touch of her caressing kiss!

II.

Dead ashes dropping from the fire,
  And dead leaves dropping in the lane;
And in my heart the dead desire
  For summer days to shine again—
  Since bitter loss brings bitter pain.

The fire dies in the dismal grate;
  The short day ends in longer night;
My heart aches with its leaden weight;
  Long grief succeeds my short delight;
  And her sweet face is cold and white!

The faded flowers are lying low;
  The sweet flower of my life is shed;
Through days of weariness and woe,
  My heart will sorrow for the dead—
  Refusing to be comforted!

III.

In dreams, in dreams, I see again
  A sweet face seen in former years,
But with no pang of sudden pain
  Or flow of unavailing tears!

In dreams, in dreams, she runs to me,
  With laughing lips and eager eyes,
Whose little grave I often see,
  Grown green with many summer skies!

In dreams, in dreams, I hear her fleet
  Familiar step upon the floor,
Who paces now, with infant feet,
  The golden pavement ever more!

In dreams, in dreams, with rapid flight,
  I rise above each fading star,
And see her in those halls of light,
  Where many little children are!

TIRED OF PLAY.

I SEE you sitting tired of all
   The joyful romp of hoop and ball,
And by your look it seems to me
That you are thinking, Dorothy.

Perhaps that thoughtful glance would say
That you are tired of children's play,
And soon, so soon, you want to be
Grown up like mother, Dorothy.

When we grow up we do not find
That things are always to our mind;
And often then we wish that we
Were like the children, Dorothy.

For we grow tired, like girls and boys,
In spite of all our worldly toys,
And have no loving mother's knee
To climb for comfort, Dorothy.

My little daughter, looking on
To life that is so quickly gone,
It is the same for you and me,
And kings in purple, Dorothy.

And tired of play, of hoop and ball,
Of books and pen, of crowns and all,
We long for that new life to be,
And joys that change not, Dorothy.

RUTH AND HER FLOWERS.

WHERE the birds and butterflies
    In the sun are flitting,
Watching them with happy eyes
    Little Ruth is sitting.

Ruth is only five, you see,
    In the charming May-time
Of her childhood's years, and she
    Makes the most of play-time.

She is fond of picture-books,
    But a warmer lover
Of the lanes, and fields, and brooks,
    And the trees above her.

Like the gems with coloured light
    Hidden in the casket,
Roses nestle, pink and white,
    In her covered basket.

Ruth is resting after play;
    Even play is tiring,
Seeing pretty things all day,
    Wondering and admiring!

Free from care we seldom rest;
    All the care she knows is
Where to find the harebells best,
    Woodbine, ferns, and roses.

A CHRISTMAS CAROL.

IT is the time when frost and snow
  Bring Christmas mirth and mistletoe,
And berries red and holly green,
And silent skies with starlight keen.

It is the time when on the tree
The shrill birds chirp for charity,
And seek for food on wintry days
Along the snow-encumbered ways.

It is the time when God in love
Sends peace on earth from heaven above,
With all the joys that shone for them
Who hailed the Star of Bethlehem!

It is the time when earth is fain
To catch the angels' song again,
Whose carol strains made glad the morn
On which the Holy Child was born!

WAITING FOR FATHER.

IN a corner of the hall
   Where the holly glistens
Bright with berries on the wall,
   Mary sits and listens.

With a sprig of mistletoe,
   There she waits demurely,
And when father comes, you know,
   She will catch him surely.

Not beneath the Kissing-bush—
   She is planning rather
To *escape* the noisy rush,
   When she kisses father.

Oh, the little artful Miss,
   Happy like the season,
Planning, plotting for a kiss,
   Can you guess the reason?

When the children, big and small,
   Crowd around to kiss him,
Pulling father, one and all,
   She perhaps might miss him!

From her nook, when they are done,
   Bright as any fairy,
To her father she will run,
   Roguish little Mary!

THE CHILDREN'S CHRISTMAS.

WHEN we were children, years ago,
 We loved the coming of the snow,
And clapped our hands with joy to see
The white flakes falling silently.

For when the whirling snow came down
On slates and chimneys of the town,
On spire, and mill, and sparkling mere.
We knew that Christmas time was near.

And with a strange and vague delight,
We listened in our cots at night,
To hear the legend, carolled high,
" I saw three ships come sailing by ! "

We used to lie awake because
We wished to peep at Santa Claus,
The friend who pleases girls and boys
With stockings filled with sweets and toys !

THE CHILDREN'S CHRISTMAS.

On Christmas Day we had a Tree
Whose splendour was a sight to see,
Laden with wondrous gifts, and bright
With small wax tapers all alight.

And oh! the laughter years ago,
The games beneath the mistletoe,
The romping children, flushed and gay,
The happy, happy Christmas Day!

BERTIE.

COME to my arms, my little son,
    And kiss away my care,
And soothe my heart and mind undone,
    With fingers in my hair!

VIOLETS.

GOD hid His violets in the vale,
    And passing breezes told the tale;
And hid like these, of precious worth,
His flowers of virtue bless the earth.

A little maiden, born to bloom
With sickness in a narrow room,
And with a smile of tender grace
To kiss the care from mother's face.

She stays at home whilst others play;
She does not find it hard to stay:
"For mother dear is ill, you see,
And baby's only good with me."

O little maiden! kind and true,
We well might learn to copy you!
O violets! blooming on the ground,
And hid, but blessing all around!

BABY COLLINS.

HIS heart is an unwritten page;
   His heart is like his face,
Where only happy charms engage
   Of innocence and grace.

And Earth and Sun, and Moon and Star,
   To him are bright and dear;
And God's good angels are not far,
   But always very near.

O you! beside whose knee at night
   He feels the soft caress,
And whispers, kneeling, robed in white,
   "Lord Jesus, keep and bless!"

O you! whose love his charms engage,
   (As in the Father's sight)
To fill that heart's unsullied page,
   What will you strive to write?

BABY.

O roguish eyes and sweet and blue!
  What shall I say or sing of you,
Whose grace it is a grievous wrong
To speak or praise in any song?

I kiss you, and I find you sweet
From curly head to rosy feet:
And all that you can crow with glee
Is worth a world of books to me.

And precious in His sight and dear
To Christ are all His children here:
And held in trust, and treasure lent,
They bring us joy from Jesus sent.

And when the lisping prayer is said,
The angels guard the little bed,
Whose eyes, beyond the starry space,
Do always see the Father's face

THEIR LITTLE QUEEN.

IT is a joyful holiday,
  When children roam the fields and play;
And baby Nell is dressed and gone
To see her cousins, Kate and John.

And birds flit by on eager wing
Past apple-orchards blossoming,
And green deep lanes, with hedge-rows high,
Steep banks, and boughs that screen the sky.

And Kate has made a hawthorn crown;
And from the bank John scrambles down,
And brings a flowering branch, and he
Fashions a rod of sovereignty.

The sceptre and the wreath are both
For tiny Nell, and nothing loth,
The maid, the dearest ever seen,
Is kissed and crowned, their little Queen!

Along the lane, and through the gate,
And down the corn-field path, in state,
Sceptred and crowned, and sweet and fair,
Borne shoulder-high, they carry her.

Oh, baby Nell, the days may be
When you will pine such friends to see,
With hearts so fond on which to lean,
So true to you, their little Queen!

A KING DEPOSED.

HIS Court is broken up, and he
　No more controls the nursery:
A King deposed, he sees to-day
His crown and sceptre pass away.

There comes, to claim his Kingdom, now
Another baby, on whose brow,
In due succession handed down,
Is placed the fallen monarch's crown.

Stripped of his honours, he will miss
The tribute of the frequent kiss
From courtier friends, a fickle host,
Who fail him when he needs them most.

Friends change with fortunes, as we know:
They hailed him King two years ago:
They placed the chairs for him to walk,
And held as wise his smallest talk.

Now this new baby takes away
His kingdom in a single day:
And in his playroom palace left,
He stands, of throne and crown bereft.

Neglected, put aside, he stands,
The sceptre vanished from his hands:
A child, among the children, he
No longer rules the nursery.

THE CHILD AND THE MOUSE.

POOR bright-eyed creature! do not be afraid!
 I will not harm you, pretty one:
My heart is not of such unkindness made,
  That I can kill for fun,
   Or give you to the cat:
   I never thought of *that*.
But you are caught, you know—what must be done?

I think a Prison must have bars like these.
  Poor little mouse! don't tremble so!
Why don't you eat that piece of toasted cheese?
  I think I'll let you go!
   For if I leave you here
   I very greatly fear
That Pussy—but she never shall, oh no!

And then there's Fred. I think Fred most unkind.
  He caught a little bird one day:

It got between the window and the blind,
  And could not get away;
    And Fred just caught it, nice!
    And Fred *loves* catching mice!
But then he kills them, too, and calls it play.

Poor little mouse! I think I'll let you out!
  I won't tell naughty Fred, not I!
But first I'll see if that old cat's about,
  For she's so sharp and sly
    Now run! or Fred will see,
    And he'll be cross with me!
But he can't catch you now—just let him try!

PLAYMATES.

THE rippling tide was deep and clear
  Beneath the quaint, old-fashioned pier;
And often there, in breeze and sun,
When days were bright, we used to run.

The fishing nets spread out to dry,
The screaming gulls, the sea and sky,
The sands, the boats, were dear to me,
And my sweet playmate, Dorothy.

We were the happiest pair alive,
And she was six and I was five;
And in our travels everywhere
We took a doll with flaxen hair.

We found a coil of rope one day,
Where Dorothy, when tired with play,
Could sit, and watch the waves, and try
To count the brown sails passing by.

And once she was not friends with me
Because I kept her doll, and she
Was cross, and would not talk, and so
We kissed, and made it up, you know.

Oh, joyful days, in breeze and sun,
When on the pier we used to run!
When first I saw the boats at sea,
With my sweet playmate, Dorothy!

HARVEST.

LAST night we saw the sunlight fall
  Beyond the gate and old stone wall,
And brighten on the stooks of wheat,
Ripe after days of brooding heat;
And in the lane we lingered long,
Then homeward turned, a sleepy throng.

Yet glad to hail the joyful day,
We rose while still the dawn was grey,
And roused the house, a merry band,
The happiest children in the land;
And all were dressed, and breakfast done,
Before the day had well begun.

The sun looked out, and quickly dried
The gleaming dew, and glorified
The broad array of clustered sheaves,
And pierced the lane's green roof of leaves,
And shone in strength, as one and all
Trooped to the gate and moss-grown wall.

And mother came, with Margery
Our eldest sister, pleased to see
The busy harvesters and hear
Our cries of triumph shrill and clear,
As heavy waggons loaded high
With rustling sheaves came rumbling by.

Late in the golden afternoon,
Yet long before the rising moon,
The last great waggon-load was piled,
And, lovely still, the sunlight smiled
Above the toilers resting there,
And those broad acres reaped and bare.

THE OLD MILL.

ONE hundred years the mill has stood:
One hundred years the dashing flood
Has turned the wheel with roaring sound,
Through foaming waters, round and round.

One hundred years: and overhead
The same broad roof of blue is spread;
And in the meadows, bright and green,
The miller's children still are seen.

And thus the world is still the same:
The sunset clouds are turned to flame;
And while we live, and when we die,
The lark still carols in the sky.

And others rise to fill our place;
We sleep, and others run the race:
And earth beneath and skies above
Are still the same; and God is love.

A PORTRAIT.

THE pictured face which here you see
  Is like, and yet unlike, for she
Had that surpassing loveliness
The artist's skill may not express;
For who with colours can convey
The glow of feeling, and portray,
As in a glass, the charm and grace
That made a marvel of her face?

And who can paint the sweet surprise,
The looks of love in lifted eyes;
And all the joy and grief at times,
Recurring like a poet's rhymes,
That are of change and beauty made;
The grief that was a passing shade;
The joy that beamed on brow and lips
Like sunlight breaking thro' eclipse?

A PORTRAIT.

Lo, when the artist strives to paint
The features of some lovely saint,
With heavenward eyes and lips apart
With speechless language of the heart,
His genius, burning to express
The beauty, truth, and tenderness,
Is powerless to depict the whole,
And with his colours fix the soul!

And so the face which here you see
Is like, and yet unlike, for she
With sweeter eyes, and brighter hair,
And life and thought, was lovelier;
I miss the soul that now is far,
And shines in heaven, as shines a star;
The soul that for a little space
Shone bright for me in her sweet face!

THE VILLAGE WEDDING.

THE weeks and months, with long delay,
  Have brought at last the wedding day;
And pealing bells, with merry din,
The joyful morn have ushered in!

And now the church begins to fill;
And all are seated, pleased and still,
While matron looks rebuke the boys
Who move their feet with shuffling noise.

And village girls, with whispered talk,
And smiling lips, have lined the walk,
And ready stand, on either side,
To scatter flowers before the bride.

And soon she comes, with modest grace,
The bridegroom waiting in his place;
The ring is on, the words are said,
They kneel to pray, and they are wed.

And shine in brightness, golden sun,
To crown a day so well begun!
And peal, and shake the ivied tower,
O bells, to hail the bridal hour!

May every blessing with them stay
That we have wished for them to-day!
And happy be the lot in life
Of loyal husband, loving wife!

THE SHOEING FORGE.

A STONE'S throw from the market town,
    Close on the lane that wanders down
Between tall trees and hedgerows green,
The famous shoeing forge is seen;
Open it stands upon the road,
That day and night is overflowed
By ruddy light that leaps and falls
Along the rafters and the walls.

And often, halting on his way,
The idler from the town will stay
To hear the sharp, clear, ringing sound,
And watch the red sparks raining round,
And the bright fiery metal glow,
While the strong smith, with blow on blow,
Hammers it into shape—a sight
To rouse his wonder and delight.

THE SHOEING FORGE.

Now in the smouldering fire once more
The bar is thrust; the bellows roar,
And fan the flame to fiercer light,
Until the metal waxes white;
Then, on the anvil placed again,
Ding-dong, the strokes descend amain;
Strong is the arm, the vision true,
Of him who shapes the iron shoe.

For thee, O reader, is the thought
That great success in life is wrought
Not by the idler as he stands
With wondering looks and empty hands,
But by the toiler who can take
Each adverse circumstance and make
It bend beneath the force and fire
Of firm resolve and high desire!

AN ENGLISH GIRL.

O FAIR as is the fragrant rose
    That in an English garden grows,
That breezes woo, that dews impearl—
O sweet she is, an English girl!

With tresses dark, or golden hair,
Blue eyes or black, she still is fair,
With all the lovely looks we see
In Jessie, Kate, or Dorothy.

The happy eyes are frank and bright,
And full of laughter, full of light;
The lips are perfect, speaking truth,
And peerless with the smile of youth.

A queen—by every poet sung—
She needs no sceptre being young,
Nor cares to wear a brilliant crown
On brighter tresses rippling down!

AN ENGLISH GIRL.

O sweet as is the stately rose
That in an English garden grows,
That breezes kiss, that dews impearl—
My love, she is an English girl!

THE VILLAGE MAY DAY.

PILED up with sacks, to yonder town
  The great mill waggon lumbers down:
Drawn by three horses, tall and strong,
The great mill waggon rolls along.

The miller's smock is clean and new,
And smart with ribbons, red and blue;
And tinkling bells on bridle rein
Have made the stately horses vain.

And every year the First of May
Is made the village holiday:
The school is closed: the children run
In meadows smiling with the sun.

And now before the mill they wait,
While some, impatient, climb the gate,
And shout with glee, when drawing near
The loudly rumbling wheels they hear.

And soon the horses loom in sight,
With gay rosettes, and harness bright,
While close beside the leader's head,
The miller walks with sturdy tread.

Long may the festive day come round
And find the miller hale and sound,
And may his goods increase, and still
The great wheel turn his busy mill.

WALTER.

FAREWELL! I hold you by the hand;
   We find it hard to part:
But love can bridge the sea and land,
   And keep us close at heart.

And when strange pictures in the blaze
   Of evening fires you see,
And sadly muse of other days,
   O then remember me!

Remember all the joy we had
   In that first glow of life,
When, full of hope, our hearts were glad
   To meet the coming strife.

Remember all the days we spent
   Beneath the happy sun,
That smiled on every good intent
   With every day begun.

Remember how we used to stand
  When evening fields were still,
To see the glare across the land
  And hear the busy mill.

Remember all our friendly talk
  In fragrant lanes at night,
When stars came out above our walk,
  And shone in silver light.

Remember when your hopes were dead
  The grief you told to me,
And how I spoke of hopes instead
  In brighter days to be.

And let the thought of this be strong
  To cheer the lonely road,
When thinking that the way is long,
  And weary with the load.

For I am still your constant friend;
  And when the dying flame
Of other love has found an end,
  My love will be the same.

AN UNBIDDEN GUEST.

A BIRD one day, as birds will do
When times are hard, came hopping through
An open window in the mill,
One day when all the place was still.

It saw, no doubt, the golden store
Of grain that covered all the floor;
But never thought, in point of law,
It had no right to what it saw.

For birds are children of the air
Dependent on the Father's care,
Who made for them His sun to shine,
And gives them food by law Divine.

And so it hopped about the floor
And dined, and came next day for more—
And every day—and on the tree
It used to sit and sing to me.

THE SINGER.

A LARK rose, rustling thro' the corn,
    With small, dusk pinions wet with dew;
The pale, pearl light of early morn,
    In skies above, was peering thro'
    The lattice bars of grey and blue.

It seemed as though the conscious air
    Was charmed to silence with the song;
I saw the brown breast-feathers stir
    With that full music, soft and strong;
    I stood and looked and listened long.

And all the waking earth was sweet;
    The brook was whispering with the breeze,
That danced away across the wheat,
    To chase the leaves and join with these
    At hide and seek among the trees.

THE SINGER.

O clear, sweet singer of the skies,
　　Teach us the worth of common things—
Seen when the world of beauty lies
　　Broad-cast around the soul that sings,
　　Borne up aloft on eager wings!

We choose the darkness and the ground;
　　We build low down beneath the corn,
And eat and live, while all around,
　　In skies above, the light is born;
　　We fold our wings and live forlorn.

THANKSGIVING.

THE village church, a quaint old pile,
  Stands where the quiet meadows smile,
Dotted with sheep, and, reaped and bare,
The stubble fields, and orchards fair.

Pleasant it was that Sabbath morn
To see the mighty stacks of corn,
And joyful on that blessed day
To feel that toil was put away.

Sweet, in the church, it was to hear
The harvest anthem rising clear,
And in those tuneful strains outpoured
To join the praises of the Lord.

For from our hearts that song arose
To Him Whose loving kindness flows
To crown with joy a thousand lands,
And bless the labour of our hands.

The anthem ceased, and still I thought
On all the mercies God had wrought:
And in my heart I took away
This lesson of that Sabbath day.

The sweetest song can ill declare
The praises of the worshipper:
The life of service must express
The heart's desire of thankfulness.

A GIRL'S STORY.

THE quaint, grey, picturesque, old grange
  Has seen three hundred years of change
With all their varying seasons pass,
And hours like sands, that thro' the glass
Of Time keep dropping, one by one;
We live, and lo! our lives are gone;
And death and change, and hopes and fears,
Fill up the measure of the years.

Here, in the pleasant gallery,
With carved oak panelled round, I see
A girl's brown eyes, and shining hair
Coiled on the shapely head, and fair,
Sad, musing face, whose charms engage
The heart like some enchanting page,
Where grief, and love, and tears prevail
In sweet Clarissa's moving tale!

A GIRL'S STORY.

A wistful, lovely face, and one
It moves the heart to look upon;
Poor child! whose eyes thro' tears of woe
Looked down a century ago,
And saw, one morning bright with May,
Her brave young lover ride away,
When by the casement on the stair
The light of life grew dark for her!

His letter told her: "thine till death!"
He fell in fight, the legend saith,
Covered with glory, and his ears
Were thrilled in death with conquering cheers
And she strove ever to endure
Her grief, and helped the suffering poor,
And lived unwedded till she died,
And now in heaven is satisfied!

CONSTANCE.

NINETEEN, with just a touch of pride,
   And all of girlish grace beside;
And rich in simple charms, a queen
By royal right of sweet Nineteen.

O vain attempt of words to show
What you by words can never know!
For who would sketch the Rose, and see
The living blossom on the tree?

But search, and say when you have seen
The face most fair of sweet Nineteen,
And find therewith the crowning grace,
A soul to match the lovely face.

And even then, when this is done,
You have not seen the sweetest one;
And Constance will remain confest
The chosen queen of all the rest.

IN THE CATHEDRAL.

To the arched and lofty ceiling
   Lordly columns rose around,
And the breathless hush of silence
   Was not broken by a sound.

Through the stained and stately windows
   Did the dying sunlight shine;
And the radiant faces on them
   Wore a rapture more divine.

But the slowly sinking splendour
   Cast long shadows through the place;
And the former glory faded
   From each fair celestial face.

Then my poet-soul indulging
   In a reverie sublime,
Sought to wander back in fancy
   Through the centuries of time.

IN THE CATHEDRAL.

Underneath the sculptured marble
  King and captain slept around:
And I knew the place was haunted—
  Knew I stood on holy ground.

When the pulseless heart no longer
  Throbs with passion in the breast,
Shall the spirit share the quiet
  Of that long unruffled rest?

Deeper grew the sombre shadows;
  And my dreamy glance, the while,
Saw a knightly train approaching
  Down the dim Cathedral aisle.

From the helmets of the heroes
  Crests and plumes were shorn away,
And the dust of weary marches
  On their dinted armour lay.

They had fought at famous Hastings,
  In the van of battle trod,
When the brave and princely Harold
  Perished on the trampled sod;

IN THE CATHEDRAL.

Dying in the hottest fore-front,
  Where the valiant ever die,
Where the chariots and the horsemen
  Wait to whirl their souls on high!

And the glad *Te Deum* anthem
  Rose in triumph from the band;
For the Norman banners floated
  Over all the conquered land!

Then the organ pealed sonorous
  Thunder from its throats of gold,
And the swelling storm of music
  Through the vast Cathedral rolled;

And the grand reverberations
  Rang responsive all around—
Thrilled along the lofty columns—
  Died away in murmuring sound.

This was but a poet's fancy,
  Born of passion and the brain:
Often does that dream of music,
  Wondrous dream, return again.

IN THE CATHEDRAL.

Often, in the twilight musing,
    Does the solitude inspire,
Till I hear the organ pealing
    And the singing of the choir—

Till the gloom before me glitters
    With the fitful gleam of steel,
And the sacred pavement echoes
    To the ring of knightly heel—

Till in picturesque procession
    Mail-clad heroes pass, the while,
In my dreamy vision, looking
    Down the dim Cathedral aisle.

MUFFLED MUSIC.

A CARELESS child, I used to sing
    Thro' halcyon days of happy Spring;
My morn of life was bright and clear:
The night drew closer, year by year.

A lonely boy, I left the rest,
And sought his side I loved the best;
A friend is sweet when foes are near:
I miss his friendship, year by year.

A dreaming youth, I longed for fame,
The honour that exalts a name;
The hope was strong my heart to cheer,
That now grows fainter, year by year.

A victor crowned, I stand alone
On hostile ramparts overthrown;
He would rejoice to greet me here:
His grave grows greener, year by year.

BEYOND RECALL.

I LEAVE the Past behind, you see;
    It glitters far behind :
The flight of fancy, wild and free;
    The happiness of mind;
The settled peace which dwelt with me;
    I leave them all behind !

I leave my Youth behind, you see,
    And hope is left behind;
I seek, in present misery,
    Some future good to find;
But this at least is lost to me,
    The life I leave behind.

I leave my Heart behind, you see,
    I sigh, and look behind,
And long for what can never be,
    For foolish love is blind;
And beauty smiles in vain for me;
    I leave romance behind.

I leave them all behind, you see,
    For evermore behind!
The leaves which flutter from the tree
    May wanton in the wind;
And False Delight may follow me,
    But Joy is left behind!

"WHEN I WAS A BOY!"

"WHEN I was a boy," the grandsire said
    To the bright lad by his knee,
"Of the victors crowned with fame I read
    Who triumphed on land and sea!
And through the years, from the deathless page,
    A summons has sounded long:
To youth, and manhood, and hoary age,
    The message is this—'Be Strong!'"

"When I was a boy"——he paused and said
    To the listener by his knee,
"Of the men who were as lights I read
    In a dark world's history!
They prized the truth, and were loved of God,
    And no fear of Man they knew:
And still, from the glorious heights they trod,
    The message is this—'Be True!'"

VAIN REGRETS.

ALAS, that sunshine of a sultry noon
   Should scorch and wither up the tender grass;
Alas, that all we love is lost so soon;
      Alas, alas!

Alas, that fragrant flowers should fall and fade,
That with the Passing summer they should pass;
Alas, that beauty in the dust is laid;
      Alas, alas!

Alas, that riches should have wings to fly,
That years of toil have taken to amass;
Alas, for breaking hearts beneath the sky;
      Alas, alas!

Alas, that on the white and wasted cheek
The hectic colour should the Rose surpass;
Alas, that death in slow decay should speak;
      Alas, alas!

Alas, that in our grief we only see
That bliss Beyond but darkly thro' a glass;
For *there* the burden of no song will be,
    Alas, alas!

THE ROBIN.

A STARVING Robin sang to me,
   With round black eyes, with bosom red,
   With bird-like grace of restless head,
Still peering here and there to see
   The white, expected crumbs of bread.

And these, in sport, I still withheld:
   So sweet it was to hear it sing,
   So sweet to watch the hopping thing,
With those quick, eager eyes compelled
   To looks of curious questioning.

But is it wise to make pretence?
   The seeming false is often fair;
   For Love is Love, though Love should wear
The mask of feigned Indifference:
   But what of unforeseen Despair?

O cruel heart that could withhold
　The crumbs on such a bitter day!
　For still the bird was fain to stay,
Half perished with the freezing cold:
A moment more—it flew away!

SONG.

"Missing the keynote which unlocks the music

THE near approach of happy spring,
  The bloom and beauty she will bring,
The sunrise on the eastern sea,
These things have lost their charm for me!

The summer days of dreamy ease,
The song of birds from leafy trees,
The sunset on the western sea,
These things have lost their charm for me!

The rapt repose of autumn days,
The chequered light in woodland ways,
The brilliant stars above the sea,
These things have lost their charm for me!

Alas, I have no heart to sing
The joys these joyous seasons bring:
He sleeps in death beneath the sea,
And life has lost its charm for me!

IN DAYS TO COME.

IN days to come I shall not hear
  The children's voices, sweet and clear,
Nor will the golden hours begin
At sunrise with their merry din!

And crowding round my chair at night,
I shall not see their faces bright:
Let me consider this, and see
What good thing else remains to me.

For though long toil had brought me then
The praises of my fellow men,
Alone and sad, I might repine
To miss the small hand clasped in mine!

Five things there are that grow not old:
The morning skies of blue and gold,
An infant's smile, a child's caress,
First love, and sweet unworldliness.

One thing is lovely with these five,
And still can keep the heart alive
When joys die out, and are not seen—
The memory that these joys have been!

Come, memory! when I sit at night
Beside the hearth, and robe with light
The lonely room, and let me see
The children climbing on my knee!

THE GOLDEN WEDDING.

IT only seems like yesterday:
  Yet fifty years have passed away
Since at the altar, side by side,
I stood with you, my happy bride.

And now our children's children stand
Close gathered round, an eager band:
Whilst we recall, with smiles and tears,
The joys and griefs of fifty years.

For we have known the cares of life,
Sweetheart, since we were man and wife:
Yet have not loved each other less
Through fifty years of happiness.

When clouds have threatened storm and rain,
The skies have always cleared again:
And fifty years have come and passed,
And brought us sunshine at the last.

And now that we are old and grey,
We trust in Him our Guide and Stay,
Our constant and unchanging Friend,
To lead us to the journey's end.

FAR APART.*

BENEATH the quaint old bridge you hear
  The waves make music as they pass;
And, winding to the elm-tree near,
  You see the pathway through the grass,
  Where we were wont to walk, alas!

The river wanders as of old
  Beneath the shade of willow trees;
The sunlit waters gleam like gold
  And ripple to the gentle breeze;
  But I am far from thee and these!

The sky bends over broad and blue,
  And, in the soft and mellow light,
You tread the lane our footsteps knew

---

* Written in memory of my old school-fellow, Frederic Ryland, and of happy years spent together at Mead House, Biggleswade—1862 to 1869.

In former days, when days were bright:
Do *these* days bring such sweet delight?

And still that lane with grass is green;
  With fragrant flowers the banks are fair;
In golden gloss and silver sheen,
  The bees still haunt the balmy air;
  But you will fail to find me there.

Again, perchance, I may not see
  The rustling rows of arching trees,
(Which lent a leafy canopy
  When we strolled underneath at ease),
  For I am far from thee and these!

Our joys forsake us. Soon does Spring
  Pass by and for the Summer call;
Soon do the birds lose heart to sing
  When fading leaves in Autumn fall;
  And Winter is the end of all.

DESOLATE.

*"Oh! who would inhabit
This bleak world alone?"*
                                        MOORE.

O FAIR and fresh the fragile flower
    That I so soon have lost:
The bud that bloomed in shine and shower
    And perished in the frost!

I miss, in all the empty 'land,
    The vision of a face:
Sad memory muses while I stand
    In this familiar place.

My life had meaning years ago;
    But lost delight is vain:
The blossom dead beneath the snow
    Can never bloom again.

What art shall charm away despair,
    Or bid remorse depart?

DESOLATE.

What winter freezes in the air
  Like that within my heart?

Ah! once I knew not how to sigh,
  With light in all my ways;
But now, alas, in darkness I
  Go mourning all my days.

Joy strays upon the verge of grief,
  And never dreams of fear;
The day of life is all too brief,
  The night of death too near.

For in her early grave she lies
  In deep, unruffled rest;
The eyelids drooping on her eyes,
  The quiet in her breast.

RONDEL.

O FOOLISH heart, thy joy may change to grief;
   The brightest day will darken being brief;
  In happy eyes unhappy tears may start;
The fairest flower, unfolding leaf by leaf,
   Must, in full blossom, with its petals part,
     O foolish heart!

O careless heart, the clouds will veil the sky;
With swift advance the winter draweth nigh,
  And soon in gloom will glowing light depart;
The song may falter with the weary sigh—
   The throbs of anguish with thy pulses start—
     O careless heart!

O happy heart, content with passing joy,
Charmed by the strains the minstrel birds employ,
  Where golden sunbeams through the branches dart,
Thy brimming chalice is without alloy—
   Without the bitterness the years impart—
     O happy heart!

THE DAYS GONE BY.

THIS is no vision from the land
   Where mortals wander when they dream,
For on the selfsame bridge I stand
   And gaze upon the selfsame stream
Sparkling beneath a summer sky,
As bright as in the days gone by!

O throbbing heart, be still and think
   Of that sweet vanished time of joy!
Still bend the grasses on the brink
   To kiss the wave, as when a boy
I stood with my lost friend beside
The flowing of this crystal tide!

Still on the banks the willows grow,
   Beneath whose leafy shade we read
"The Talisman" and "Ivanhoe,"
   Till passing horsehoofs seemed the tread
Of knightly riders as they went
To join some Norman tournament!

And half afraid were we to look,
  Lest haply we might not behold
Their snowy plumes which proudly shook
  On helmets shining bright with gold:
The branches rustled in the trees
Like banners blowing in the breeze!

But all its former charm has gone
  From this sweet spot where willows wave:
The river, ever rippling on,
  Brings but to mind *his* distant grave:
And my sad eyes shall look in vain
To see that long lost friend again!

FAITH AND WORK.

THIS gospel is more true and sweet
   Than all beside that men declare;
It is as light and strength and heat
   In hearts that waste with dark despair.

We have no time to moan and sigh,
   With fears assailed, and filled with grief;
For each and all beneath the sky
   One happy way will bring relief.

Work, though the heart should throb with pain;
   Toil on, and be of better cheer;
Work, with both hands, and with the brain,
   Busy and bright, and keen and clear.

The lot of all beneath the sky,
   We live by faith, assailed with grief;
We have no time to moan and sigh;
   We trust in God, and find relief.

CONSCIENCE.

DEEP down in every human heart
  By storms of passion stirred,
The springs of purer impulse start—
  A pleading voice is heard.

It whispers sweet in childhood's years,
  And firmly speaks in youth,
When what we lose is worth our tears,
  But not our love of truth.

This voice rebukes the harsh resolve
  When manhood's pride is high;
And day by day, while days revolve,
  It teaches age to die.

This voice, O God, that pleads within,
  Incline our hearts to hear,
Till in Thy sight, made free from sin,
  Through Christ, we all appear.

LET US BE TRUE.

LET us be true, the young and strong,
  And, waging battle with the wrong,
Stand, clear of darkness, in the light,
And brave the world, and do the right.

From day to day, from year to year,
Let conscience speak, and reason hear,
And action seal—though pain and grief
Oppress the heart beyond relief.

Though we should die for it—the truth
Is brighter on the brows of youth
Than crowns of gold that glitter fair
With crime and falsehood written there.

And void of gloom the days shall be
When age and weakness muse and see
The days of strength that shine afar
Where truth was like a guiding star!

"THE EVIL DAYS."

BEFORE the Evil Days draw nigh,
   When pleasures pall on dead desires,
And grey funereal ashes lie,
   To mark the place of perished fires:

Before the sun is hid in gloom
   By clouds returning after rain,
And light forsakes the joyless room
   No joy shall ever light again:

Before the morning fails to bless
   With melody of waking birds,
And words of winning tenderness
   Lose all the charm of tender words—

Because they fall on listless ears,
   That through the watches of the night
Hear voices from the vanished years
   With sorrow and with no delight:

"THE EVIL DAYS."

Before the sad, despairing soul
   Looks out in vain from darkened eyes
To find her lost immortal goal,
   And wails her wasted energies,

That grasped at every gilded toy,
   And every flower upon the sod,
When happiness, without alloy,
   Was waiting at the hands of God:

Before the silver cord is loosed,
   And mourners go about the street,
And lips are still in death that used
   To turn to bitter all of sweet:

O seek the Lord, whose love draws nigh
   In yearning pity, lest the door
Should shut and mock the awful cry,
   "Too late! too late! for evermore!"

"DIEU ET MON DROIT."

"Dieu et mon droit" was the *parole* of the day at the Battle of Gisors, in which Richard I. defeated Philip of France. It has ever since been retained as the royal motto.

"GOD and my right!"
In the front of the fight
That blazon shall haughtily blow;
And burning with ire,
Like billows of fire,
Our bravest shall sweep on the foe!

Like pillars of rock
That scornfully mock
The might of the turbulent main,
In phalanx of iron
Our ranks shall environ
The standard they charge for in vain!

"DIEU ET MON DROIT."

  The soldiers of Gaul
  In myriads fall
'Neath the sword of the Lion-heart King;
  " Dieu et mon droit,"
  'Mid the thunder of war,
Swells high o'er the clangour and ring!

  In crimson and gold
  Our banners still hold
That motto of ages gone by;
  For God and the right
  Still Wellingtons fight,
Or Nelsons, victorious, die!

MARIANA.

THE path we trod was broad and bright,
And far from any realms of night:
His kiss was burning on my lips:
And still, thro' all this blank eclipse,
I think of that unclouded light.

And all his words to me were sweet:
The ferns and grasses at his feet,
　The leaves and branches overhead,
　Were fairer for the words he said,
In grace and beauty more complete.

And broken vows have taken root
In my sad heart, and borne their fruit
　Of hopes that droop in barren ways,
　And die, remembering brighter days
Before the lips of love were mute.

I pluck the blue Forget-me-not,
He planted in my garden plot,

With sky and sun beholding him:
And these may perish, waxing dim,
When I forget as he forgot.

THE HEART'S WINTER.

O STILL, though faith and love were sold
　　For pride of place, or birth, or gold,
The throstle's note would warble clear,
And Spring would bless and crown the year!

And in the early Summer's morn
The glowing light would still be born;
And Autumn's sun would sink and die
Behind the flushed and silent sky!

And dark by night, and bright by day,
The world would keep its constant way;
And years would pass, and speed their flight,
With changing seasons, day and night.

But what, when faith and love were sold,
So sweet as these could we behold?
O clouded earth, no longer dear!
O death in life, to linger here!

MINOR CHORDS.

THE lips may smile when joy is dead;
   The garlands grace the loveless tomb;
The full-blown flower is soonest shed;
   The brambles trail where roses bloom;
   One cloud can veil the sun in gloom.

The joys of life are quickly gone;
   The longest day in darkness dies;
The face most fair to look upon
   Must fade at last from loving eyes;
   Death does not heed despairing cries.

The day-star sheds no beam of bliss
   On him who in a dungeon wakes;
The parting follows on the kiss;
   The vows of love the lover makes
   Are broken with the heart he breaks.

The weary poet walks apart:
   The sunlight on the river gleams:

The waves make music in his heart,
　And lull the dreamer into dreams:
　How dark the disenchantment seems!

The major chords one moment swell:
　To fairer realms my fancies stray:
In fields of fadeless asphodel
　I hail the light of endless day:
　"The former things have passed away."

CONFESSION.

MY love is like a Rose that grows
   Low down and hid, where no one knows;
A Rose that blossoms on the tree,
Where those who look will never see.

My love is like a Star at night,
Among a thousand stars of light;
A single star that shines for me,
When those who look will never see.

And like the Star, and like the Rose,
My love is mine, and no one knows;
And, bright with light and beauty, she
Is sweet alone, and sweet for me.

GREY AND BLUE.

WE heard the nightingale repeat its lulling love-song to the night;
And all the leafy lane was sweet with roses red and roses white;
And breathless was the fragrant air, and deep the peace that brooded there.

And hearing all the words I said, the changing colour flushed her cheek;
The roses white and roses red were mingled as she heard me speak;
While thro' the trees a sweeter strain of mellow music went again.

"Your eyes," I said, "are brighter, love, than stars that shine in summer skies;
The sapphire blue of skies above is mirrored in your sweeter eyes;
The brilliant stars and skies of blue find all their beauty merged in you!"

"Alas!" she said, "your words are vain; the darling
  of departed days
Would laugh to hear this pretty strain when she
  recalled the sweeter praise
That you, the poet, wrote of her, whose eyes were
  grey, whose face was fair:"

"In breathless beauty as they shine,
  The stars make sweet the summer skies;
But sweeter that sweet face of thine
Is made by loving light divine
    Of sweet grey eyes!"

"If painter, love, could paint aright,
  With faultless skill, your eyes of grey,
With all their wealth of subtle light,
The world would throng to see the sight
    From day to day!"

"If poet, love, 'with soul of fire'
  Should his sweet praises seek to bring
(Sweet with the music of his lyre!),
  His voice, for very wondering,
    Would cease to sing!"

"An idle song!" I made reply, "that wakes no
    echo in my breast;
But, whilst the bird is warbling by, ah! listen to
    this last and best;
A song of your blue eyes and sweet, where light
    and love together meet:"

"Blue eyes or grey? grey eyes or blue?
Which seem the sweeter now to you,
O lover, as you wait for her,
Whose eyes are blue beyond compare?
        The while you wait
        Beside the gate,
To hear your darling come this way—
Grey eyes or blue? blue eyes or grey?
Which are the sweeter, lover, say?

"Blue eyes or grey? grey eyes or blue?
I render praise where praise is due:
As down the garden-walk I hear
A sweet, swift footstep drawing near,
        As on the gate
        I lean and wait,
To hear my darling come this way—
Grey eyes or blue? blue eyes or grey?
Her eyes can turn my night to day!"

The moon sailed thro' the blue abyss as down the
 lane alone I went;
Upon my lips her parting kiss, and in my eyes a
 proud content;
And stars peeped out in summer state above the
 garden and the gate.

FIRST LOVE.

THERE is no second love like this:
  For there is something that we miss
In second love, however true:
And this it is, the first was new.

And I could die for her, and she
Could smile in death to die for me:
But hearts are frozen, old, and grey,
When passion burns itself away.

And second love is not the same:
It is as though the heat and flame
Should glow and sparkle in the fire
Where wasted ashes now expire.

The lips are cold, the lips we kiss:
It is the fresh delight we miss
In second love: the first was new,
And was and is for ever true.

TWILIGHT.

IT is the sweet and tender grace
  Of sorrow in a lovely face,
When the bright eyes are brimmed with tears,
That yearns through all the vanished years.

For, though long years have passed away,
I still recall that parting day
When here, with breaking hearts, we stood
In this dim twilight of the wood.

The winding pathway is the same;
The oak, on which I carved her name,
Still casts its shadow over me;
And still——ah! what is this I see?

The pale face lifted to my own,
The sad, sad lips that made sweet moan,
Unconscious of the future years
When other eyes would fill with tears.

THE ROSE.

WHERE sleeping sunlight all the day
   On that green lawn reposes,
One rose for me will wait and stay
   Among her sister roses—
   One rose of all the roses!

Across the lawn one summer's day
   (Where golden light reposes),
My loving eyes beheld her stray,
   With blushes, through the roses—
   One rose of all the roses!

And on the lawn the self-same day
   (Where sunlight sweet reposes),
I lost my heart and strolled away
   To dream about the roses—
   One rose of all the roses!

When on the lawn some future day
   A fairer light reposes,

THE ROSE.

My steps, by happy chance, will stray
  To claim, among the roses,
    One rose of all the roses!

THE TRYSTING PLACE.

GREY walls, green grass, and ancient trees,
　　Twisted and gnarled; and over these,
Bright rays of sunlight streaming fair,
Like joys that bless a world of care.

What is it that I find so sweet
Where gloom and shining glory meet,
Where arching trees their branches spread,
Where roses blossom, white and red?

A light, light footstep in the fern:
What sight is this that I discern,
Most fair of all, where all is fair?
What bliss is mine, beholding her!

It is the lovers' trysting-place;
And here, when meeting face to face,
Where roses blossom, white and red,
The world outside is cold and dead.

MY LOVE AND I.

I FIND it sweet to think of her,
   Who seldom thinks, perchance, of me;
For many lovers find her fair,
   And many rivers seek the sea.

I find it sweet to think of her,
   For thoughts by day bring dreams by night,
Wherein no sorrow comes to share
   Or shadow my supreme delight!

I find it sweet to think of her,
   Whose gracious praises make me strong
To win the crown those poets wear
   Whose love and passion speak in song!

I find it sweet to think of her,
   And of her words I found so sweet;
And, like a charm to lull my care,
   My lips their music still repeat!

MY LOVE AND I.

I find it sweet to think of her,
   And, through these ashen autumn days,
A sense of peace pervades the air,
   Though leaves strew thick the woodland ways.

I find it sweet to think of her,
   And though my heart may haply break,
When hope surrenders to despair,
   The pain were sweet for her sweet sake!

I find it sweet to think of her,
   Who *sometimes* thinks, perchance, of me,
Though many lovers find her fair,
   And many rivers seek the sea.

SUNSET.

IN grass-grown, sheltered ways and green,
  Where gleams of glory glance between
The rustling leaves that shroud the lane,
I walk and talk with Lil again.

I hold my love by both her hands:
The sun that lights a thousand lands,
Will rise for me, will rise again,
Will search for Lil and search in vain.

The dying day will linger still,
With silver stars, for love of Lil:
The breeze will murmur and complain
Thro' all the dark, deserted lane.

And looks of love in lifted eyes,
As now, to-night, will then arise,
With happy thoughts, with thoughts of pain,
With Lil no longer in the lane.

EVENING.

I LOVE the veiled and quiet light
   Of evening on the verge of night,
When from the hedgerow nest is heard
The last faint chirping of the bird.

I love the rose-flushed cloud that sails
Where western splendour pales and pales,
And sweeter still, the smiles that rise
With looks of love in happy eyes.

O what were life of love bereft!
And what of joy in life were left,
If love should die and leave us here
To miss and mourn a brighter sphere!

I love the sweet and tender light
Of evening ere it grows to night,
And, sweeter still, I love to see
The face most fair of all to me.

THE BIRD'S MESSAGE.

A LITTLE bird, a little love,
   Flew down to me from skies above,
And lighting on my window-sill,
A sweet surprise, it sang of Lil.

The crimson feathers round its throat
Were stirred with every thrilling note
Of carol music, soft and clear:
A sight to see, a song to hear.

It came but once, and flew away;
But now I know, from day to day,
That we are close, though far apart —
Close to each other, close at heart.

A little bird, a little love,
Came flying down from skies above,
And perching on my window-sill,
It tapped the pane with news of Lil.

TREASURES.

WE take delight in little things,
  In written vows, memorial rings :
We find the treasures of the earth
In little things of little worth.

Why were we born beneath the stars
That glow for us through cloudy bars,
Revealing all the heaven above,
If we were never born to love?

I cannot tell, I only know
The seasons come, the seasons go,
And all the days are bright and fair
And golden days because of .her.

We live in love of little things,
Of lockets, letters, treasured rings :
We find the riches of the earth
In little things of little worth.

BETROTHAL.

WE walk where stars are shining fair,
  With no one else in sight:
To-morrow I will speak to her,
  I dare not speak to-night.

But if, by chance, my words could frame
  The heart's desire aright,
(The heart that loves no other name),
  Then I might speak to-night.

Ah! sweet, what answer can you give?
  O tears that glisten bright!
And will you trust me while you live,
  And love me from to-night?

THE GLADE.

THE gay leaves dance, the sunbeams glance;
   The glade is sweet with shine and shade;
With flushing cheek, you hear me speak—
   With eyes averted, half afraid;
   Shadow and sunshine in the glade.

With lips that meet, the shadows fleet;
   The glade is filled with golden light;
From dewy brakes the music wakes;
   A thousand strains in one unite;
   The heart of Nature throbs with might.

We hear the song the birds prolong—
   The mating birds in leafy bowers;
And thou art mine, and I am thine,
   And love, the light of life, is ours—
   The marriage altar crowned with flowers.

WAITING.

THE rose he plucked, when first we met,
    To set and fasten in my hair—
The faded rose is treasured yet:
    And hope is stronger than despair.

The lips of love will not betray,
    Though hope should strive with many fears
The heart of love, from day to day,
    Is changeless through the changing years.

We live in hope—we trust and wait:
    The stars that glitter through the night
Will faint and fail; the golden gate
    Of morning will disclose the light.

The rose he gave, when first we met,
    To blush with beauty in my hair—
The withered rose is treasured yet:
    And hope is stronger than despair.

HOPE DEFERRED.

THE tender trouble of her eyes
   Is born of hope deferred; the tears,
In witness of her grief, arise
   From day to day, through all the years.

And often in her sleep at night
   Are visions beautiful to see;
And in the darkness there is light:
   And this is half her misery.

For dreams of vain delight are one
   With weary waking thoughts of pain,
For when the happy night has gone
   The **dreary** morning comes again.

And joy and sorrow fill her eyes
   When friends surround her; sudden tears,
When quiet and alone, arise
   From day to day, through all the years.

A WITHERED ROSE.

WE lingered in the meadow croft:
  We saw the summer moon aloft
In silver light: the earth, the sky
Were not so full of peace as I,
Whose days have lost their tranquil tune
Since love can die so soon, so soon.

He plucked a fragrant rose, and there
He set the blossom in my hair,
And clasped me close, and whispered low
Of changeless faith, which now I know
Inconstant as the changing moon,
Since love can die so soon, so soon.

The nightingale was warbling clear
In liquid notes: I did not hear
The witching music of the bird;
His vows of love I only heard.
O sad and sweet that night in June!
Since love can die so soon, so soon.

A WITHERED ROSE.

I keep the rose, whose darkened hue
Recalls the joy which once I knew,
That gathered colour day by day,
And brightness, till it fell away,
With hopes like faded petals strewn,
Since love can die so soon, so soon.

I keep the rose: the time may be
When I with firmer heart shall see
Its withered leaves, nor sigh to find
In life's calm eve new peace of mind,
Though clouds obscured its early noon,
Since love can die so soon, so soon.

STARLIGHT.

I SEE the white road winding down
   Through starlit meadows to the town;
The years return, the years that were;
I think of these, remembering her.

The river glistens far below;
Beyond the bridge the branches throw
Their trembling shadows, faint and fair;
I lean and look, remembering her.

The rushes in the river-bed;
The leaves that bicker overhead
With winds that kiss them unaware:
I love them well, remembering her.

The lane is sweet with tender light,
With rain-washed roses, red and white,
As when we used to linger there;
I pluck a rose, remembering her.

But foolish lips forbore to speak,
From day to day, from week to week;
The years went on, the years that were;
I walk alone, remembering her.

RECOMPENSE.

ONE flower alone, of all the flowers,
    Sweet with the summer sunlit showers,
One blown queen blossom on the tree,
Was more than all the rest to me.

And one proud face was passing fair.
One face alone, beyond compare:
It was, alas! as lovers know,
My heart of hearts that told me so.

The wind crept down the garden walk
And stole my blossom from the stalk:
My passion met with her disdain:
I loved her, and I loved in vain.

And so I gave—the world was wide—
Scorn for her scorn, and pride for pride:
And still, alas! I found that she
Was more than all the world to me.

CONSUMMATION.

AH! is it well that, fresh and free,
  The brook should babble through the lea,
    And, waxing broader, wind between
    The willow-bordered banks and green,
To gain the salt and bitter sea?

Ah! is it well that I should see
The folded rosebuds on the tree,
    And find, from day to fairer day,
    The leaves unfold and fall away,
Till my last rose is lost to me?

Ah! is it well that there should be
Such silence over land and sea,
    Such rapt repose in brooding skies,
    Before the thunder-clouds arise,
And all of former quiet flee?

Ah! is it well, when thus to thee
Thy lover bends the suppliant knee,

That thy coy lips should still refrain
From one kind word which blesses twain,
Which speaks thy sweet consent to me?

FINAL FAITH.

O SWEET and bitter, sad and true!
    I love you still and only you:
Betrayed, forsaken, is it strange
That love is love and cannot change?

O vain regret! the days depart:
And, day by day, the faithful heart,
That loves you still, is full of pain
For days that will not come again.

O fond and fickle, false and fair!
Do you recall the days that were,
And think of these without a thrill
Of pain for one who loves you still?

O last and first! the songs of love
Are full of faith on lips above:
And, having loved you, is it strange
I love you still and cannot change?

PARTING.

THE stars will light the vault of night
    And we shall meet to sever:
For love is dead, and faith has fled,
    For ever and for ever.

O loved and lost! with bitter cost,
    With all we prize and treasure,
With sad surprise, with streaming eyes,
    We pay for fleeting pleasure.

The sun will rise in happy skies,
    And in familiar places,
Where first we met, the sun will set
    And miss remembered faces.

But was it sweet to kiss and meet?
    For now we meet to sever,
To kiss and part, with pain of heart,
    For ever and for ever.

FIRELIGHT.

I GAVE the wealth of love for dross
   Of falsehood, and I suffered loss:
For who shall tell the worth of love,
The light on earth from heaven above?

I sit and think of this, and see
The buried past that used to be:
And, in the dusk, the dying fire
Is flaming, ready to expire.

Love that is true is like the light
Of sun and stars, for ever bright:
Love that is false is like the fire,
The flames that flash and then expire.

And love that sells itself for gold
Is dear to buy, and cheap to hold:
And love that gives itself for love
Is light on earth from heaven above.

RONDEL.

AT thirty years, it is enough for me
   To know I am not what I hoped to be!
It is enough, storm-beaten on the plain,
To view the splendid heights I cannot gain—
Low down to miss the music of the spheres—
      At thirty years!

The half of life has passed, and half remains:
One effort more, O soul, to break the chains
Of circumstance! to fill this page of Time
With characters of glory, and to climb
The steep ascent, with songs in place of tears,
      At thirty years!

The clouds will pass; the sun will dazzle thro'
On rose-flushed pinnacles that pierce the blue:
O deep disgrace, to loiter on the plain—
Irresolute, to grieve at toil and pain—
To be the slave of sloth and sordid fears,
      At thirty years!

SONG.

WHAT day of days will dawn for me,
  On what far-off to-morrow,
When I shall cease to think of thee
  With sorrow, endless sorrow?

What faith in happiness to be,
  What comfort shall I borrow,
When all my life I think of thee
  With sorrow, endless sorrow?

The day of death will dawn for me,
  That knows no dark to-morrow,
When I shall cease to think of thee
  With sorrow, endless sorrow.

LUX IN TENEBRIS.

O LOVE! O sorrow! O delight!
   The seasons come and go:
They bring the day, they bring the night,
   They bring me joy and woe.

I raise the chalice gleaming bright
With clustered roses, red and white:
   With tears that overflow,
With sorrow void of all delight,
   I drink the cup of woe.

The sun will rise, the sun will set,
   In clouded skies and clear,
And hope forlorn, and vain regret,
   And grief will fill the year.

And love supreme will tarry yet,
One star, when all the stars have met

Made manifest and dear :
One star, when all the stars have set,
Through all the changing year!

"NO CROSS, NO CROWN."

THE poet who has charmed the world
  May in a garret pine for bread;
And he who bears the flag unfurled
  Must in the van of battle tread
  Amid the dying and the dead.

They only rise who first aspire;
  The martyr wears the gloriole
When he has triumphed in the fire:
  And they who make the skies their goal
  Must plume the pinions of the soul.

"No cross, no crown;" there is no choice;
  We climb the rugged steep with pain,
But on the summit we rejoice:
  Hereafter we shall not complain
  Of loss which was the price of gain.

A thousand forces lie in wait
  To drag us from our purpose down:

But shall we, on the verge of fate,
Forsake the pathway of renown—
Forego the cross, and lose the crown?

THE CITY'S LITANY.

O LORD, how long with naked feet
   Shall little children roam the street?
And pray, with starving lips unfed,
"Give us this day our daily bread!'
Till pitying hearts redress the wrong,
   O Lord, how long?

O Lord, how long shall sin and shame
Blaze upward like an altar flame,
   With human souls for sacrifice?
   How long shall they for whom the price
Of death was paid to ruin throng?
   O Lord, how long?

O Lord, how long shall mercy strive
In vain to save these souls alive?
   How long shall discord vex the earth,
   That heard glad music at her birth,
When stars began their choral song?
   O Lord, how long?

O Lord, how long shall men proclaim
The Infant born at Bethlehem?
   When in the great cathedral's shade
   The sad, small children shrink afraid,
Reared into crime by cruel wrong;
     O Lord, how long?

O Lord, how long shall darkness brood
Above the weary multitude,
   Till light dispel the night of sin
   And bring the heavenly kingdom in?
In faith we pray—our faith. is strong—
     O Lord, how long?

JUBILEE NATIONAL ANTHEM.

(Tune: "Rule, Britannia.")

OUR country, in her pride of place,
   With green fields smiling on the deep,
Makes ready, with a festal grace,
   The year of Jubilee to keep.
Hail, Victoria! Victoria, on whose crown
Fifty happy years look down!

Through all the cities of our land
   The lighted streets shall mock the day;
On jutting cliffs and headlands grand
   The fires of Jubilee shall play.
Hail, Victoria! Victoria, on whose crown
Fifty shining years look down!

O Empress-Queen! From every heart
   A blessing shall be breathed for thee—
Thy people's love the brightest part,

The jewel of thy Jubilee!
Hail, Victoria! Victoria, on whose crown
Fifty golden years look down!

A REQUIEM.

GONE, in the dawn of life,
  Before the heat and strife—
"Whom the gods love die young"--
What shall be said or sung,
With tears that fall between,
While yet the grass is green
  Above his early grave?

What new sweet forms of speech,
What lyric words, can reach
The height of his renown,
Or weave for him a crown?
What Requiem shall be said
Above our dearest dead,
  Laid in his early grave?

Let Memory, hand in hand
With Love and Sorrow, stand,
Each with a wreath of flowers,

A REQUIEM.

Gathered in twilight hours,
And let the three unite
Their vigils day and night
　Beside his early grave!

And first let Memory tell
Beneath the tolling bell
His work was nobly done!
His life, though scarce begun,
Was filled with earnest days,
That follow him with praise,
　To crown his early grave!

And next let Love declare
How sweet, and good, and fair
His soul, and heart, and mind!
How true a friend and kind!
And what bright hopes are crossed,
And earthly fame is lost,
　Hid in his early grave!

And last let Sorrow say
We mourn him night and day!
Yet while with holy trust
We guard his sacred dust

A light from Heaven begun
Falls brighter than the sun
  To bless his early grave!

Let night winds whisper sweet,
And birds their songs repeat!
And there let violets grow,
And roses white as snow!
And thro' the days and years
Let dews descend like tears
  Above his early grave!

EMBLEMS.

THE shining light discovers
   The deepness of the shade;
We sigh the more in sadness
To hear the song of gladness;
The quarrel of the lovers
   Seems harsh when peace is made;
It is the light discovers
   The deepness of the shade.

A breath creates the bubble,
   Dissolving at a breath;
In merry peals and knelling,
The selfsame bells are telling
Of blessing and of trouble,
   Of bridal, birth, and death;
So floats and fades the bubble,
   The bubble of a breath.

The faithless swallows leave us
   When gloomy days begin;

EMBLEMS.

We live and love together
Through glad and glowing weather:
The smiling lips deceive us
  With words that woo and win;
Our friends betray and leave us
  When darker days begin.

The fair and fragrant roses
  Are found on thorny stems;
We hate the sins we cherish;
In pain our pleasures perish;
Our foolish nature closes
  With evil it condemns;
Our hands are full of roses,
  But wounded with the stems.

The tide with useless swelling
  Resounds upon the beach;
We pass the day in sorrow
And dream of joy to-morrow;
Our hopes are ever dwelling
  On bliss beyond our reach;
The tide of life is swelling
  To die upon the beach.

The autumn winds are sighing
  Where yellow leaves descend;

Our joys are evanescent;
The future mocks the present;
The hours are winged and flying;
 This life in death will end;
The mournful winds are sighing
 Where withered leaves descend.

Is there no type of heaven
 For us on earth below?
The stars their watch are keeping:
For sleepless eyes and sleeping
Their gentle light is given
 As through the gloom they glow:
So may we find in heaven
 The light we seek below!

"VIVE L'EMPEREUR!"

(A Reverie in the Chapel of the Invalides, Paris.)

"*VIVE l'Empereur!*" Methinks I see
    The stern grand face before me now:
The steadfast eyes, the raven hair
    Sweeping the broad majestic brow!

"*Vive l'Empereur!*" Upon his lips
    The smile of triumph proudly sits,
As the unclouded sun surveys
    His hosts encamped at Austerlitz!

"*Vive l'Empereur!*" in thunder rolled
    Through the dense mist of sulphurous smoke,
As on the squares at Elchingen
    Ney's furious squadrons fiercely broke!

"*Vive l'Empereur!*" The challenge cry
    Rose high on Jena's battle field:

What time before our bayonets bright
   The routed Prussians backward reeled!

"*Vive l'Empereur!*" Wrapt round with flame
   Great Moscow's mighty ramparts glow:
Whilst the long columns of retreat
   Stretch far across the waste of snow!

"*Vive l'Empereur!*" At Montereau
   Still frowning stands the famous Bridge:
How ceaselessly the iron storm
   Beat on that blackened shattered ridge!

"*Vive l'Empereur!*" "*Vive l'Empereur!*"
   The cry goes ringing to the sky
As on the volleying British squares
   Ney's horsemen dash, recoil, and die!

"*Vive l'Empereur!*" Behold the end
   Of all his splendour, pomp, and pride:
A sea-girt rock to mark the spot
   Where the earth-shaker drooped and died!

"*Vive l'Empereur!*"—but let that pass!
   Where bannered trophies mutely wave,
Our souls a solemn silence keep
   Beside the mighty conqueror's grave!

THE CROSS OF THE LEGION OF HONOUR.

(Spoken by a Veteran of the Old Guard to a youthful Conscript.)

I TROD the white and scorching sands
    Beneath the fierce Egyptian suns,
What time the Arab riders swept
    With whirling sabres on our guns!

I saw the flag-ship's flaming wreck
    Rush up aloft with thunder sound;
The billows of the boiling bay
    Were black with fragments all around!

I led the stormers to the breach
    At Acre on that fatal day:
"*Vive l'Empereur!*" our bayonet charge
    Soon cleared a passage through the fray!

At famed Marengo—sore beset—
    Our drooping eagles fluttered low:

Like music pealed the crashing charge
   Of Kellerman upon the foe!

My eyes beheld the morning sun
   On tented Austerlitz arise;
The glowing splendours of the dawn
   Flung sudden glory through the skies!

The battle smoke at Jena hung
   In sombre masses overhead;
The bearskin shakos of the Guard
   Towered high above the Prussian dead!

It was in Russia that I won
   The decoration of the Cross;
In shrouds of snow our bravest slept:
   What glory could redeem their loss?

Like famished wolves upon our track
   The yelling Cossacks gathered near;
One savage sought the Marshal's breast:
   My lifted arm received the spear!

Look, Conscript, at this precious Cross—
   Napoleon placed it where you see;

A sling sustained my shattered arm —
   And thus the Emperor spake to me:

"My comrade!"—and the light of praise
   Shone in the proud imperial glance—
"Wear this in memory of the deed
   Which saved a life so dear to France!

"The Cross becomes thee well, *mon brave!*"
   And, as I bent in reverence low,
His hand went up in grave salute,
   And raised the *chapeau* from his brow!

I heeded not the wild applause
   In stormy thunders rolling on:
I only heard those thrilling words;
   I only saw Napoleon!

Now harken, Conscript, to this last
   And darling boon that I must crave——
See none disturbs this sacred Cross
   When I am laid within my grave—

That when the ringing blast of doom
   Shall rouse the sleepers from their rest,
I, Sergeant Victor, still may wear
   The Cross of Honour on my breast!

THE OLD GUARD AT WATERLOO.

COMRADES, remember Austerlitz!
   What cause have we to fear
Their fiercest shock of crashing horse
   When Bonaparte is here?

Remember how the Cossacks charged:
   Those stern words thrill me yet:
How sharp they rang: "*Halte! genou terre!
Croissez la baïonette!*"

Remember how we climbed the Alps,
   Whose summits gleamed with snow:
How gladsome lay the smiling fields
   Of Italy below!

Remember old Marengo:
   How red the great plain ran!
No British horsemen ever charged
   Like those of Kellerman!

No Marshal brave as Kellerman,
   The valiant and the true,
Who carved a path to victory
   And bore the eagles through!

Remember grim old Davoust,
   Bronzed by Egyptian suns:
How shook the ground at Auërstadt
   Beneath the thundering guns!

Remember Moscow's mighty walls
   Wrapped round with fiery flame:
How fast upon our drooping ranks
   Those wolfish Russians came!

Remember famous Montereau:
   The havoc and the death:
How swift the squares were swept away
   By the hot volley's breath!

  *   *   *   *   *   *

Hark—how the shouts of "Victory!"
   Come swelling on the gale:
But shall the Veterans of France,
   Who fought at Jena, quail?

The furious onslaught we await
　With dauntless mien and high:
The grand Old Guard can never yield:
　The hour has come to die!

MARSHAL NEY.

(Shot December 7th, 1815.)

HIS glorious body lies at last
   In a dishonoured grave:
The Hero of five hundred fights,
   "The bravest of the brave!"

At Elchingen, in fire and smoke,
   Long raged the doubtful fray:
How swift the Austrians fled before
   The thunder-charge of Ney!

Old Erfurt's granite bastions grim
   Of his great name shall tell:
How trod beneath his trampling horse
   Her staunch defenders fell!

But Magdeburg a sterner tale
   Has of her Gallic foes:

What time upon the battle breeze
　　The *pas de charge* arose!

At Deppen still, with whitened lips,
　　The story shall be told:
How on the fated Prussian squares
　　His proud battalions rolled!

His conquering columns, rushing on,
　　Spurned the red heaps of slain:
Those Russian soldiers never fought
　　At Koningsburg again!

To Waterloo, his latest field,
　　Great France her Hero calls:
In vain his furious squadrons swept
　　Upon *those* flaming walls!

There set Napoleon's mighty star
　　In night of blackest dun:
That star which rose on Austerlitz
　　A sudden, dazzling sun!

The Garden of the Luxembourg—
　　O saddest scene of all!—

Beheld the bravest son of France,
  Her grandest soldier, fall!

Alone in that December dawn
  To death he proudly trod:
His voice rang out the firing-word
  Which sent his soul to God!

Shot like a traitor! thrust away
  In a dishonoured grave!
The Hero of five hundred fights!
  "The bravest of the brave!"

PLEVNA, 1877.

THE cloud of horror darkly falls
Around thy scorched and shattered walls:
    Yet lift thine eyes cast down,
    And take thy fadeless crown!

Thy Hero, Ghazi Osman, he
Whose name is great with victory,
    Henceforth thro' all the days
    Of Time is thine to praise!

Thy deathless Hero, great alone
In simple duty nobly done:
    How nobly and how well
    Let future Ages tell!

For when shall deeds like his expire?
They fill the hearts of men with fire!
    And fadeless is the crown
    By Ages handed down!

THE KING'S MESSENGER.

THE red glow of morning had tinged the grey sky,
  When across the wide country, my charger and I,
Hot pressed by the roundheads, rode reckless and
    fast ;
But three miles to Oxford—how long will it last?

The wall rises grimly—the torrent is deep—
I drew my breath harder, and dashed at the leap;
One shout of defiance—one touch of the spur—
We're over!—ho, crop-ears, come on if ye dare!

Their steeds spring out wildly, and plunge in the
    flood ;
Each roundheaded rider is rolling in mud :
I doffed my plumed hat, with a parting "good day ;"
Then, wheeling my charger, rode swiftly away.

SACRED POEMS.

"FOR SO HE GIVETH HIS BELOVED SLEEP."

SWEET is the silent night when day is done;
  Sweet is the starlight: sweeter than the sun;
And sweet in death the dreamless slumber deep:
"For so He giveth His belovëd sleep."

Our eyes wax weary when the daylight dies,
And sweet is slumber to our weary eyes;
And softly do the shadows round us creep:
"For so He giveth His belovëd sleep."

The landscape, lovely with the light of spring
No blessedness to broken hearts can bring,
In which the anguish only wakes to weep:
Wherefore, "He giveth His belovëd sleep."

The vain delight, with canker at the core,
The sharp distress, shall visit them no more;
To joy or grief no more their pulses leap:
"For so He giveth His belovëd sleep."

In place of pain He giveth perfect ease:
A restful haven after raging seas—
Where angry waves and winds no longer sweep:
"For so He giveth His belovëd sleep."

Sweet is their sleep beneath the summer skies;
Sweet is their sleep when storms of winter rise;
And sweet the watch which guardian angels keep:
"For so He giveth His belovëd sleep."

But He Who gives them sleep shall give them grace
To rise in rapture and behold His face,
When that last trumpet echoes loud and deep:
Till *then*, "He giveth His belovëd sleep."

"THOU KNOWEST NOT NOW!"

OUR troubles fade, but leave their trace;
    And years of toil and care
With lines of sorrow mar the face
    That once was fair!

O would that we could feel and know
    That grief is sent in Love,
To wean our hearts from earth below
    To God above!

O would that we could understand,
    And calm would follow strife!
O would our eyes could see the Hand
    That guides our life!

For then our feet would choose the way
    That now we strive to shun;
And, full of praise, our hearts would pray,
    "Thy Will be done!"

"SEEK YE MY FACE!"

SEEK ye My face. The world will bring
   No real joy to thee;
For joy is of the living Spring
    That flows from Me.

Child of My love! hast thou no care
   To heed this call of Mine,
And in thy human life to share
    The Life divine?

Behold, I left My throne for thee,
   My Father's house above,
And stooped to all thy misery
    In boundless love!

And I have sought thy love's return:
   And saved by dying grace,
The love of all thy soul should yearn
    To seek My face!

"FOR ME TO LIVE IS CHRIST, TO DIE IS GAIN."

THE faltering fingers touch uncertain strings:
　Of love, of earthly love, the poet sings—
Of love, when doubt assails, so quickly slain;
O words of love which speak diviner things!
　"For me to live is Christ, to die is gain."

The gold of autumn turns to ashen grey;
The dirge of hope remains from day to day
　The burden of our songs, the sad refrain;
Till smiling lips at last have learnt to say,
　"For me to live is Christ, to die is gain."

John, leaning on the bosom of the Lord,
And ever listening for the whispered word,
　Found rest and peace in weariness and pain;
Love is its own exceeding great reward;
　"For me to live is Christ, to die is gain."

In Jesus the Divine and human meet,
The harmonies of life are made complete,
   The wailing minors cease to vex the strain,
The varying chords awake in music sweet—
   "For me to live is Christ, to die is gain."

When shadows deepen in the dying light,
When sunset glory fades in gloomy night,
   His shining stars shall make my pathway plain,
His hand in mine shall guide my steps aright,
   "For me to live is Christ, to die is gain."

"I STAND AT THE DOOR AND KNOCK!"

"I STAND at the door and knock!"
It is bolted and barred;
    I have stood many years,
    I have waited with tears,
And thy heart is still hard;
The door to My summons is bolted and barred.

"I stand at the door and knock!"
I am waiting for you;
    I have loved as a Friend
    Who loves to the end,
And the cold and the dew
Descend on Me waiting in patience for you.

"I stand at the door and knock!"
Will you open to Me?
    In mercy and love
    I came from above,
And I died on the Tree;
And will you not harken and open to Me?

"I stand at the door and knock!"
I am bringing the light;
   There is darkness within
   And sorrow for sin ;
And My presence is bright
With the joy of Salvation, and I am the Light.

"I stand at the door and knock!"
And My summons is heard;
   For conscience has made
   Thy spirit afraid ;
And thy sorrow is stirred,
And mourns for the past, and My summons is heard.

"I stand at the door and knock!"
My Redeemer come in!
   I open the door,
   That closes no more
In rebellion and sin ;
My Lord and my Life! my Redeemer come in!

"OUR FATHER."

THY ways, O God, though hid, will tend,
  Marked out in love, to some good end;
Be Thou our Guide, and in the night,
Lest we should stray, be Thou our Light!

We come as children, needing all
The sweetest words that sweetly fall;
We hear Thy voice and, hearing, we
Are fain in faith to follow Thee!

We once were vain of heart, and found,
Strong in ourselves, no certain ground;
But now, at last, have learnt and seen
How sweet it is to trust and lean!

O lead us, we are prone to stray;
Be Thou our Guide, be Thou our Way;
O let us hear Thy voice, and we
Will trust Thy love and follow Thee!

"GIVE ME THINE HEART!"

"GIVE Me thine heart!" When life was young
    That summons gently came,
With Jesus in the songs I sung
    The sweetest name.

And God still called. The endless day
    Was in its early noon,
With hours that beckoned far away:
    It was too soon.

O love Divine! the grief, the tears,
    The Life laid down for me,
And my return of sinful years,
    Estranged from Thee!

O late repentance! I resign
    What Thou hast made Thine own,
And all my heart's best love is Thine,
    And Thine alone!

"LOVEST THOU ME?"

Lovest thou Me?
  Are friends growing cold
  And losing their hold
  On affections set free
From loving the creature to love the Creator, to centre in Me?

  Lovest thou Me?
    The sheep that were Mine
    Were ninety and nine;
    But one I could see
Far off on the mountain in danger, one sheep that was dear unto Me.

  Lovest thou Me?
    The hireling will sleep,
    Nor care for the sheep;
    The hireling will flee;
But I am the Shepherd Who sought thee, My sheep that had wandered from Me.

Lovest thou Me?
 When the morning was bright,
 And no shadow of night
 Had fallen on thee,
Thy heart was not happy, forgetting thy Saviour,
 forgetful of Me.

Lovest thou Me?
 When the light of the day
 Began to decay,
 And thy trouble could see
No gleam in the darkness, in mercy that darkness
 had fallen from Me.

Lovest thou Me?
 Thou art weary of sin,
 And the light enters in;
 And happy for thee,
Thrice happy the angels of heaven for one who is
 coming to Me.

Lovest thou Me?
 O answer My call!
 And the burden will fall,
 And thy spirit set free
Will rest from its labour and sorrow, and find its
 redemption in Me.

L

IN SIMON'S HOUSE.

SHE kissed, she bathed the Saviour's feet
  With tears, she wiped them with her hair;
Bowed down with grief, the faith was sweet
  That filled her heart with prayer.

They looked, reclining at their ease,
  And knew her, and their scorn increased;
The haughty Scribes and Pharisees,
  They watched Him at the feast.

For their self-righteous souls sufficed
  The scorn that would as lightning fall;
O Friend of sinners, Jesus Christ,
  Thy grace is free for all!

He speaks in pardon. Who but He
  Could so confirm the faith that trod
In paths that turned from misery
  And sin, and turned to God?

OUR HOME ABOVE.

FOR all who sigh with pain opprest,
   Whose hearts are wounded sore,
There is a home of joy and rest,
   There is an open door.

That door of mercy open stands—
   And free from grief and sin,
And glad at heart from many lands,
   The nations enter in.

O happy in a happy place!
   They lay their burdens down—
The cross they bore a little space
   Exchanging for the crown.

O faces pale and worn with grief!
   O eyes that weep below!
O blessed hope of that relief
   Which God will soon bestow!

FORGIVENESS.

O GOD, forgive the years and years
  Of worldly pride and hopes and fears;
Forgive, and blot them from Thy book,
The sins on which I mourn to look.

Forgive the lack of service done
For Thee, thro' life, from life begun;
Forgive the vain desires to be
All else but that desired by Thee.

Forgive the love of human praise,
The first false step in crooked ways,
The choice of evil and the night,
The heart close shut against the light.

Forgive the love that could endure
No cost to bless the sad and poor;
Forgive, and give me grace to see
The Life laid down in love for me.

THE NEW EXCELSIOR.

*"On the roaring billows of Time thou art not
engulfed, but borne aloft into the azure of
Eternity. Love not pleasure ; love God."*
SARTOR RESARTUS.

LET us ascend, why do we linger here?
   Lo, in their marshalled millions, sphere on sphere,
Stars mount on stars, like joys that have no end!
Lo, crushed by crowding sorrows, year by year,
   Vain is our life below, the years we spend;
      Let us ascend!

O soul cast down and sad, hast thou no wings?
Why on the dust of earth and creeping things
   That choose the darkness does thy vision bend?
The heaven of heavens is thine; the King of kings,
   And Lord of lords, thy Father is and Friend;
      Let us ascend!

O still, thro' stress and storm, a little while,
Be ours, Eternal hope, that we may smile,
  Though pains take hold of life, and sorrows rend!
Not as the hopes of earth that here beguile,
  But ours to whisper sweet—when earth shall end—
    "Let us ascend!"

www.ingramcontent.com/pod-product-compliance
Lightning Source LLC
Chambersburg PA
CBHW032137160426
43197CB00008B/678